Gift of a

Gift of a Cross

An exploration of the Easter Story from the
Triumphal Entry into Jerusalem,
through to the Empty Tomb and beyond.

A resource for reflection, worship
and personal prayer.

Pat Marsh

British Library Cataloguing in Publication data

A catalogue record for this book is available from the British Library

ISBN 1 85852 297 8

First published by Inspire
4 John Wesley Road
Werrington
Peterborough PE4 6ZP

Printed and bound in Great Britain by
Biddles Ltd, King's Lynn, Norfolk

Dedication

For the many people who have helped me to journey
towards my own resurrection; with special thanks to Tricia.

Acknowledgements

I am deeply indebted to my dear friend, the Revd Chris Beatson, who kindly spent time with the manuscript and gave advice on scriptural inaccuracies within the text.

I also give thanks to the retreat houses of Launde Abbey, Green Pastures and The Open Gate who supported me by providing prayerful writing space to facilitate the birth of this book.

Lastly, I am grateful to Dr Natalie Watson of Inspire for her continuing support, understanding and encouragement, without which this book would not be in print, and to my many friends, far and wide, who have sustained me through my own 'Calvary times'.

I thank all of them, not only for their help with this book but also for the way that my fellowship with them draws me closer to Christ.

Pat Marsh
October 2005

My poetry is born from prayer,
is in itself a prayer;
and through the tumbling of the words
onto the printed page
seeps
into the stillness of my soul
and leads me deeper
into prayer.

Contents

Sacrifice

(The Crucifixion)

Surrender

(The Last Few Hours)

Resurrection

(The Empty Tomb and the Risen Lord)

Implications

(Postscript for Today)

Preparation

The Triumphal Entry to the Upper Room

The Lamb

John 12.12-15

Every ounce a human,
every inch divine,
not for the first time
turning the world's values
upside down,
by opting to enter Jerusalem,
choosing to meet his people's praise,
on the back of a simple colt;
a beast of burden
this day bearing
the burdens
of all the world.

Thronged by the noisy crowd
in town for the Passover feast,
crying Hail, Hosanna,
Blessed is he,
waving symbolic victory palms
and forming a carpet
as for a king,
worshipping him who came to save
though not in the way they understood,
unknowingly greeting
the Lamb,
the Lamb of the Passover ritual.

Crowd Control

Luke 19.28-38

Cheers, smiling faces,
shouts of joy;
exultant corridor of dancing palms
forming a pathway for the donkey
as he plodded onwards
with his load
towards Jerusalem,
more leaves beneath his hooves,
strewn in welcome
on the stony path:
spontaneous red-carpet treatment
for a donkey
and the coming King.

He wasn't used
to giving rides
and he wondered
if it was always as much fun as this.

Hosanna! Hail! Rejoice!
Electric atmosphere
of adulation and respect.

But a week
can be
such a very long time
in history:

five days later
their shouts
would change
to Crucify!
Crucify!

It's difficult
not to be controlled
by the crowd
when you're in the midst of it.

Turning the Tables

Luke 19.45-46

There was no doubt about it:
the man was mad.
They spoke of him
as a man of peace;
the whole of Jerusalem
worshipped him,
speculated
this was the one
who might be the Messiah,
but that day
he turned all those concepts
upside down.

I've never seen such anger:
clearing the tables,
sweeping the merchandise onto the floor,
then knocking them over,
smashing them up
and all the while accusing us
of making the temple
a den of thieves.

Who was he
to boldly tell us
we were wrong;
we'd made our pitch there for years:
people have to buy their sacrifices somewhere
and there's good trade here
at festival time.

We were only making a living,
providing a service, you might say:
where else
would they get their doves?

Just an ordinary day
until he came along;

now I need to find a carpenter
to mend my market stall.

Alabaster Jar

Mark 14.3-9

Trickling down his forehead,
the damp, sweet perfume,
cool, refreshing, invigorating,
flooded his senses
with the fragrance of her love:

offering all she had,
in an act of confession and repentance
that she could not bring herself to voice,
the woman
broke open the alabaster jar,
and anointed the Christ
by pouring the perfume over his head.

Aroma of nard
pervaded the room,
filling the nostrils of those who watched
with more than a heady hint
of the extravagant nature of the gift;
a costly balm
more normally saved
to prepare a body for a burial
but given this day as sacrifice,
a token gesture for all her sins;
for those who seek
to be forgiven
need to repay in equal measure
and this was the costliest offering
she could make.

There were those
who rebuked the wastefulness
of what they saw as a misplaced gesture,
but Jesus
loudly silenced them,
pronounced forgiveness for her sins,
accepted the magnitude of the gift
and used the anointing
to foretell his coming death:

her costly sacrifice
preparing the way
for his.

Role Reversal

John 13.1-5

I felt embarrassed at first,
uncomfortable,
didn't want his hands
to touch my filthy feet,
resisted
this display of love,
wanted it to be I
who was serving him,
felt undeserving
that he should play
the servant at my feet
but later
I could see the lesson here:
no service to others too mundane,
too inconvenient or menial,
no giving too great
when we understand
the one it is we serve.

Not a pretty sight,
my big flat fisherman's feet,
hardened by years of weathering,
soiled by the mix of grime and sweat
that comes from days
of tramping the paths of Palestine
in open shoes.

Not a pretty sight,
or smell.

But he willingly took up a towel,
lowered himself to kneel
and lovingly washed them clean.

In my memory
I feel that water again right now;
the touch of his hands upon my feet,
the fresh, reviving, cool caress
as the dirt of days
was bathed away;
my feet enlivened by his touch,
toes dancing with ecstatic wonder
at this demonstration of his love.

I remember the reverence
with which he touched my skin,
the time that he gave
to complete the task,
soothing away
not only dust and dirt
but also my deep discomfort
and as my weary feet
became revived, refreshed
I understood:
no service too distasteful
when we recognise
the face of him
whom we are serving.

My feet came fully alive
that night.

Forewarned

Luke 9.21-22

He talked about if often enough,
tried to forewarn us
of what was about to happen,
but none of us
could quite absorb it;
didn't want to, you might say
and you'd be right,
but actually
couldn't, either;
how could we:
such an impossible idea,
a hair-brained concept,
that he might die
and then in some incredible way
come back again.
The whole idea
was completely outside our experience,
beyond our given understanding
of death, of life,
of Jesus
and what he was about.

To think of him dying was bad enough,
we didn't even want to consider that,
let alone believe it:
the last three years would have been in vain,
life would lose its meaning
without him,
or so we thought.

Believing in his death
was tough enough,
but coming back again,
being raised,
as he put it;
who could get their head around that?

The Bread

Matthew 26.26

With gentle, reverent hands,
hands
that were to be broken and mutilated,
bloodstained and shattered
by the imprint of the nails,
with those very same hands
he lifted up the bread
and looking at the twelve
said 'this is my body'
and tearing it apart with his hands
he symbolised
what was to happen:

this is my body
to be broken
for you.

and he passed the bread
around the table
one to another
saying

take, eat,
receive my body into yourselves

I do this
for you

remember me
when you break the bread.

He Gave Thanks

Matthew 26.27-28

He gave thanks.

He asked God
to bless the cup,
lifted it high
for all to see,
looked at it with love
and then gave thanks,
saying we were to drink it,
share it;
all of us.
Red wine it was:
he gave thanks for it
saying it was his blood
to be poured out on the cross
for us,
sealing the promise of God,
the promise of forgiveness
for all people
and all sins.

Can you believe that?
He knew
what he was going to face
in the coming twenty-four hours,
the only one who did;
he knew the agony
he was going to journey through,
anticipated
the pain that would wrack his body
to the death:
he knew all that
with a vivid understanding
denied to us

and still he gave thanks,
rejoicing
that his blood,
his costly sacrifice
would seal a new covenant for God's people,
opening the way
for them to receive
his grace.

He gave
thanks.

The Rooster

John 13.36-38

Before the rooster crows,
three times
you will deny me,
he said.

I remember saying,
No, no Master,
not I:
I'll never deny you.
You'll always have my loyalty.

He'd turned my life around, you see,
this man.
I used to be a fisherman:
a hard life, that was.
And now here I was
following him,
Jesus,
healing the sick,
teaching people a radically different way to live,
feeding thousands with a young boy's picnic,
fishing,
this time for people.

I walked on water towards him once,
so when he said
You will deny me
three times
before the cock crows,
I said
No Lord,
not me.

Bread and Wine

1 Corinthians 11.23-26

Bread and wine.

For his memorial
he chose the ordinary, everyday;
the normal means of nourishment
and sustenance,
the foods we need to live:
a simple loaf of bread
and a cup
of the juice of the vine.

He was always doing that,
taking the everyday stuff of life,
coins, sheep, yeast, seeds,
and using it
to help us recognize God
in our midst.

And now he was saying
when I am gone,
after I've been put to death,
I want you to gather together,
often,
and share
this simple meal of bread and wine
to remember
I am still in your midst,
will be amongst you,
even
after I have died:
this meal
will give you all you need.

Then came the surprise;
he tore the bread apart with his hands
and said remember
that my body was broken
for you,
and he lifted up the wine and said
remember
that my blood
was shed for you:
he didn't say
look at this bread
and recall how we fed five thousand
or look at this wine
and remember how they danced at the wedding feast
after I changed water into wine.

He didn't say
don't forget my miracles
and the wonderful things we did.

He said instead
keep reminding yourselves
of my death,
of what I'm about to do
for you,
because that's the crucial thing:
my redeeming death
the crowning moment
of history.

Bread and wine,
my body and blood,

broken
and poured out for you,

because I love you.

Thirty Coins

John 13.21-30

Chosen:
one of the twelve,
in the group
yet hardly known to them;
an outsider,
not of Galilee
but chosen nevertheless.
How readily he betrayed a friend
for thirty pieces of silver.

Taking the place
of the honoured guest at supper,
accepting the special portion,
affirming the Master's love
yet in the intentions of his heart
already a betrayer.

Pilfering petty cash for years,
the keeper of the purse
who kept some
for himself.

It was clear
from all Christ voiced,
in the ripples of tension everywhere,
they were going to arrest him anyway:
what harm in using the situation
to line his pockets
a little more:
second nature to Judas,
to weigh up financial deception.

And knowing
what he was about to do
and being prepared
to die for him,
Jesus commanded
'Do what you have to do'
and Judas went out
into the night
to betray his friend
for thirty pieces of silver.

Submission

Gethsemane to Golgotha

Olive Grove

Luke 22.39-44

I needed to pray:

now, more than ever before,
I had to pray.

Supper was over,
the last we would share
this side of the resurrection.
Night was descending,
the hour of my betrayal
painfully close.
I knew
that I had to pray
and ask others to intercede.

We had to find
a safe spot;
isolated, undisturbed,
somewhere I could wrestle with God,
grapple
with all that tore me apart inside.
Gethsemane
was the spot:
not a place anyone else would go
at that hour of the night.

I left the three
sitting under a tree,
their backs against the rough bark,
their prayers soaked in the pungent smell of olives:
I asked them to watch and to wait
and to pray.

Down on my knees,
the tension and turmoil intense within,
too tight to voice,
the whole of my guts in a rigid knot,
sweat pouring out of my hands and face,
red like blood,
muscles and sinews tense
with anticipation:

did God really want me to go through this?

Take it away,
this cup of suffering, Lord;
I can no longer bear the agony
tearing me apart inside:
how can anyone face death
when they know the hour of its coming;
how does anyone find strength
to go through torture
when they're given advance notice?

I would do anything
for the Father;
but this ...
I really wasn't sure
if I had the strength of body, mind and spirit:
I certainly knew
I couldn't do it
from within my own resources

so once again
before a pivotal moment
in my ministry
I had to pray.

Please take this cup away from me.

But the olive grove
echoed loud with silence:
never had I felt so distant
from the God who was my Father,
never so lonely,
and yet I knew
it had to be.

Yet not my will
but yours
be done.

Arrest

John 18.3-4

It began as a faint whisper,
imperceptible,
almost inaudible
in the far distance,
gently breaking the stillness of night
and to begin with
faint glimmers of light
shimmering orange
behind the shadows of olive trees
and long before the disciples
understood the approaching noise,
before the growing whisper
had risen to crescendo,

Jesus fully realized
what was about to happen.

The tramp of a whole battalion of boots
crashing through undergrowth,
the clash of cold steel weapons against leather
and the volley of soldiers' voices
was suddenly upon them;
the bright hot glow of flaming torches
fuelling the atmosphere of tension
but, the agony
of the earlier Gethsemane moments
gone,
Jesus reflected
only calm acceptance:
his coming death
his very reason for living.

Whom are you looking for?

The Kiss

Matthew 26.48-50

Beneath the olive trees
two men kissed,
embraced each other
in the failing light:

for one,
a kiss of farewell
hidden
behind a veil of friendship,
for the other,
a gesture of acceptance
delivered in a kiss,
a kiss
which spoke of a love
that could endure
anything,
even betrayal.

Shlam, Rabbana.

Hello Judas.

Travesty

John 18.14

There never was
a case to answer,

nothing made sense
about the arrest of this man,
his trial
a trumped-up
travesty of justice
driven by corruption,
self-interest,
priests
who should know better.

They judged him
by their own values
and found him to be wanting
as their sins
stood out in sharp relief
against the openness of his love,
his principles
clashed loudly
with their profits.

The case
of the High Priests
versus Jesus of Nazareth.

Whatever the false litigation,
popularity was his crime:
he was simply becoming
too well liked,
the strength of his following
undermining their power.

He knew of the rife corruption,
rich pickings lining their pockets
from the temple traders;
why else overturn the tables
in the holy place?
And if these stories about resurrection
began to gain ground,
the ones that had grown
since he raised Lazarus,
and all people
aspired to live as one big family under God,
who knows what would happen then;
their wealth, the priests',
would be
all for nothing.

He had
to be stopped:
there'd be nothing short of a riot
if this following grew
and then the Romans would intervene
and all would be totally lost.

They were doing the people a favour:
better to let one man die
than to have the whole nation destroyed.

It never did make sense, this trial
but they had to make the charges stick,
any charge would do;
the verdict:
already decided.

Twofold Tragedy

Matthew 27.3-5

The corpse of a broken man
swings eerily,
silently,
from a tree.

Judas,
one of the twelve;
a noose around his neck,
driven to kill himself
in irreparable anguish
at the outcome of his greed,
his conscience exchanged
for the paltry sum
of thirty coins.

He had not meant it
to end like that;
not in the Master's death:
no, never that.

He ran,
ran like a man possessed
through the twisting streets,
raced through the temple door,
wild horror
in his eyes:

I have sinned:

betrayed
an innocent man.

I did not know ...

But his words
hung helplessly in the air
as the priests
just laughed:
So, what do we care?

Hitting the floor with force
the noise of silver impacting marble
matched the explosion
inside his mind:
it was
too late,
too late to make amends;
it had all gone
very wrong.

And as the coins
clattered, rolled, spun wildly
across the temple floor
Judas ran
and ran
until he could run no more;
past the crowds,
away from it all,
beyond the city walls,
as far as adrenalin would take him.

And all he could see
through his tear-stained eyes
as he blindly stumbled along
was the face of Jesus
as he kissed him;

such a peaceful face,
a remarkable man.

And all he could hear was
'he called me Friend';
again and again
it echoed, resonated
in his head,
Friend,
my Friend.

The corpse of a man
hangs heavily
from a tree.

What tragedy;

but greater tragedy still
that he took his life
too soon,
that he thought himself
unforgivable,
that he never saw
or understood

the promise of Christ's death,

the meaning
of the Cross.

Denial

Matthew 26.69-74

It was the anger that threw me off guard,
pitched my nerves off balance,
sent me on the defensive:
don't much like anger, you see.
I've always been one
for keeping the peace,
whatever the cost to me.
Such a simple, unguarded moment.
I denied it,
denied him,
said I wasn't a disciple of his,
and before the words had left my tongue
almost immediately
I hated myself,
couldn't believe
the things I heard myself voicing.
I was lying
big-style.
He was everything to me.
I loved him
so very much.
He turned my whole life completely round;
and not just me:
he was changing lives
wherever he went,
healing the sick, teaching forgiveness,
loving everyone,
whoever they were,
whatever they'd done.

Funny that.
I denied him.

A couple of days earlier
when he'd hinted I'd deny him
(three times, he said)
I told him he was wrong,
said I'd die for him first,
I loved him that much.

Funny that.
In the end,
that's what he did for me.

Disclaimer

Matthew 27.24

The whole thing
defied belief:
there was no crime
of which he could find him guilty;
he couldn't understand
why they'd arrested him
in the first place.

This man was no common criminal,
there was something about his whole demeanour
and his calmness under questioning
that marked him out as different:
he'd never seen a man
so completely devoid of aggression
in the face
of such massive injustice.

The peace of the man
touched Pilate
deeply.

The people made their choice:
release Barabbas
and crucify
the one from Nazareth.
Crowds are easily incited,
he supposed,
and he had to appease the people,
but something
didn't feel right about this.

Pilate sent for water
and pointedly washed his hands
before the watching throng.

I wash my hands of this.

I am innocent
of the blood of this man:
the responsibility
rests with you.

And still they cried:

Crucify.

Kingdom Joke

Matthew 27.27-31

They draped a floor-length cloak
round his shoulders;
purple, it was,
a rich, deep, regal colour
and they fashioned a crown out of thorns
and forced it onto his head.

It was their way
of mocking
this so-called King,
the sovereign they did not recognize,
their making fun of him
a mask
to live behind,
hiding their need to question
the validity of the trial.

They were enjoying it now
in a sick, sadistic way,
laughter
hiding their insecurities,
concealing their personal doubts,
helping disclaim responsibility
for what they'd been ordered to do,
the torture concealed
behind a joke:
somehow it made it acceptable.

'King of the Jews'
was carved on the sign
they finally stuck
above his head
but nobody really dared to believe
he might be.

It was all
a bit of a joke:
best not to question
whether they believed
what they were laughing at.

On the Road to Calvary

Luke 23.26-27

I just got swept along
by the crowd,
in the midst of the throng
and yet alone within my feelings:
it's hard to be truly yourself
inside a crowd;
you get carried along
on the tide of the noisiest opinion,
your own strong feelings
drowned out, suppressed,
hidden behind an outer layer of conformity,
of wanting to belong;
safe, personal,
well out of harm's way,
hid from the anger
of those within the mob
who would oppose you.

It horrified me,
being swept along
within the identity of that crowd,
but something compelled me to stay,
to follow to the end.
I wanted to have no part of it;
the injustice of his torture
and his death.
I wanted to cry out
against the beatings
and the nails
but shock
held me mute,
shock
gripped me in silence,
shock kept me in the crowd.

Only with hindsight
could I see

I was an integral part
of that following crowd:
it was my sins,
our sins,
that were torturing him
on the road to Calvary.

Do Not Weep

Luke 23.28

You become
dangerously desensitised to death
when you see too much of it,
complacent
about another crucifixion party
trudging past your door;
the familiarity of the scene
softening the hard edges of the grief
that wants to scream from you,
recoil
against this barbarous form of justice:
after a while
it becomes
just another cross,
just another criminal
and you don't weep
any more
even though public outbursts of grief
are part of the culture here;
familiarity
dulls the senses
and Jesus was not the first
to shoulder a cross through these dusty streets
on the way to his lonely death.

But the execution of Jesus
was different,
this day was different;
this day
no one could suppress the tears,
the anger,
the raw distressing grief
that welled up from our guts;
this day

we cried, lamented, openly wept
as we followed him
along his path,
our tears giving voice
to the sorrow of the world.

Somehow
he found the strength
to straighten his back,
force himself up
from the crippling stoop
that develops
under the weight of the wood
and somehow the courage
to defy the military:
as he stopped on the path
and crossed to us,
took the initiative
to come and say,

women of Jerusalem,
do not weep for me.

It was as if he knew
there was a greater purpose
to this pain:
the hour of Jerusalem's greatest grief,
the midst of his personal agony,
and he just quietly said
Do not weep.

I can see the peace in his eyes,
and I can hear again his voice:

Do not weep for me.

Simon of Cyrene

Luke 23.26

Here, you –
carry this cross,
they said.

I didn't have much of a choice,
feared for my life
if I refused:
not best to argue
when a Roman's pointing a spear at you.

He couldn't carry it
one more step,
the Christ;
that much was clear:
the strength
was all beaten out of him,
not the courage, mind,
he still had oceans of that,
but the stamina, power,
physical strength
to carry that gallows across his back:
all that
was gone.

Maybe I looked strong,
I'm a biggish bloke you see,
or possibly something in my demeanour
angered the passing soldiers
but either way
I had to do it:
it was me who they ordered
to carry his cross.

And so I did:
the heaviness
impressed itself on me,
the weight of the wood
digging into my back,
deadening the muscles
across my neck,
bruising my shoulders
with punishing pain
and all the while
the hot sun burning down on us.

The crowds were jeering,
taunting, mocking me,
making me feel a perpetrator
of the crime,
but I was just
an innocent bystander
dragged unwittingly centre stage
into an awful moment
in history.

I'd only come in from the country
for festival time.

I watched him
stumbling bravely on
without a word of complaint,
completely broken in every way
but beaten in spirit,
never

and the punishing pain
jolting its way
right down my spine
wasn't unbearable
any more.

This was nothing
compared to what he was going through,
going to.

It was a privilege
to shoulder his cedar tree cross:
though I was carrying his cross
he was carrying more.

Costly Love

John 19.16-17

The crushing weight
of the sins
of all the world
upon his back
and not even one of them his;
what grace
to accept that load,
what grace
to shoulder the cross
and bravely walk,
what overwhelming love
as he stumbled towards Golgotha;
human energy visibly draining,
divine energy empowering,
enabling him to love
to the very last breath,
still reaching out to others
as he journeyed to
and through
the cross;
a loving glance here,
a kind word there,
a look of peace,
a tender gaze
in every lonely moment
on the unforgiving road
to Calvary.
Never was a walk
so bitter
and so sweet;
love
never so diamond-hard
and costly:

divinity at its best
facing humanity at its worst;
the carpenter God
giving absolutely everything
to restore us
to himself.

What love:

what costly love.

Sacrifice

The Crucifixion

The Crucifixion Tree

Luke 23.32-38

Before this day
his roughened hands
might have fashioned me into a thing
of usefulness or beauty;
he worked with wood you see,
a carpenter from Nazareth,
and before this day
he might have crafted me
into something special.

But today was different.
This was the day
that was to be
the turning point of history.

This day
my wood was to form
his crucifixion cross;
his blood was destined to drip
onto my timbers,
mingle sacrificially
with my sap.

This day they were to nail him to me
and leave him to die,
his only crime, speaking the Truth.

Pinned to me by savage spikes,
the cross I formed
bore the tragedy
of all the cruelty and sin
that man could inflict on man.

It was to be
my saddest hour,
this Friday noontide.

And after
he'd pronounced it
'finished'
with his dying breath,
and the spear had pierced him,
just to make sure,
and the earth had trembled and violently shook,
the ones who loved him
lowered his body
reverently
and I stood
empty
on the hill,
splattered red,
the holes that housed the nails
and the pattern of his blood on me
the only evidence
of the purpose they had put me to.

Well Rehearsed

Mark 15.22-24

The soldiers begin their task
with clinical precision
and matter-of-fact indifference;
crucifixion's a well-rehearsed procedure here,
whoever the victim.

Even before the nails
secure him to the cross
our Lord is already
embracing the world
in forgiveness,
strong arms of the carpenter
stretched out
with a calm acceptance
of this cruel and undservèd death,
the death that will slowly claim him
once these measured, meticulous preparations
are complete.

Nails, hammer, hoist.

Love, death, salvation.

The Man with the Nails

Matthew 27.35

The soldier stepped forward
with the nails.

It was all in a day's work to him:
death by crucifixion
was not uncommon in those days.
It was a messy job:
the sticky blood
often spurted scarlet all over him
as nail bit into flesh
and crushed through bone,
and the scream
usually shivered right through him
as the spike hammered home,
there was always a scream,
but someone had to do it;
in a way
he supposed it was a short straw
but he didn't much care:
there were harder tasks
and it was just a job he had to do.

The soldier
stepped forward with the nails.

Did he know
that Jesus was forgiving him,
even as he brought down the heavy hammer
to deliver the callous blow?

Nail Maker

Colossians 1.16

It is I
who made the metal for the nails,
me who grew the timbers
for the cross,
my hands that shaped the ground
into the hill
and my desire
that all should have free will.

It is I who made the hands
through which the nails drove,
the bones that splintered
and the blood that flowed;
I created flesh men ripped apart
and I desire
that all
should have free will.

I created all that is and will be
and every day
I am creating still.
I put myself
upon the cross

and still I know

love must allow
free will.

Fullness

Colossians 2.9

And the fullness of God
hung on the cross

and the visible image
of the invisible God
bled on the cross

and the mind and the body
of the living God
were tortured
on the cross:

divinity stepped down
inside humanity,
made himself vulnerable,
exposed himself
to the very worst
humanity could inflict
upon itself,
that he might bring
peace
between heaven and earth;
experiencing the very depths
of all that we might ever know
in order to redeem sin
from the inside.

And the fullness of God
allowed himself
to be stripped of dignity,
drained of life,

that we
might stand holy and blameless,
forgiven and freed,
before him.

He did it
for us.

What love.

What incredible love.

Jocular Game

John 19.23-24

They hardly noticed
the blood splashing red onto earth
as the dice
rolled, tumbled
and bounced over dusty ground;
the Christ
haemorrhaging
above them:
they only had eyes
for the wooden blocks
which twirled, spun,
danced across ground
in a game of chance:
engrossed in the gamble,
oblivious to the scarlet wine
dripping by their feet;
laughing, cheering,
trying to predict
how the dice would fall;
each one focused
on taking the robe of Jesus home
as if it were a schoolboy trophy
far removed from the drama of death;
the jocular game
a pleasant pastime
to shield them from the reality
of the evidence of cruelty
hanging
over their heads.

The Passion

John 19.25-30

I wonder which was worse:
the crippling mental torment
of terrible rejection
and undeserved abuse
or the cold steel piercing pain
of sharp nails hammered home
through innocent flesh.

I wonder which was harder
to take upon yourself and bear:
the smarting, stinging punishment,
inflicted lash on lash,
the price for all our sins,
or the raw, exposed, humiliating
hanging on the cross,
longing for the sweet release of death.

What tortured conversations
screamed and echoed in your head,
unheard, unseen,
behind the narrowed eyes
through which the peace of your acceptance
shone out upon your foes?

Such brave empowering by the Father
for his Son.

And I wonder which was tougher:
forcing your broken body
to go the extra mile
or buckling beneath the knowledge
that the crippling cross you shouldered

should be rightly borne by those
who whipped you unrelentingly
as you fought to find the strength
to walk your lonely road.

Which was the greater battle:
watching the haunted eyes of Mary,
paralysed by shock,
or bearing the physical torture
of the last three final hours
of your three-and-thirty years?

Did the riveted eyes of Mary
sustain you through the evil,
as you now empower us?

Forgiven Thief

Luke 23.39-43

I couldn't
take my eyes off him.

I'd watched
a fair few criminals
meet their death
on a wooden cross,
it was the norm hereabouts
for justice to be meted out that way
and now it was my turn:
I'd gone
one crime too far
and it was my body
hanging high above the crowd,
my muscles
screaming out in pain,
my wrists
breaking under my hanging weight,
my chest
suffocatingly tight,
the breath impossible to draw.

What a fool I'd been
and how bitterly I regretted it now.

What a tortured walk
of weighty memories
from the courtroom to the hill.
I hated it:
hated the soldiers,
hated the people,
hated myself.

But I'd known the rules
and I broke them:
I deserved
to be strung up
and left to die.

But him:
he was different.

I couldn't take my eyes off him.

I'd heard all the talk that was going on
about the word of his teachings, healings, miracles,
the wonderful things that were said of him,
the suggestion
he might even be
the Son of God
but, as with most things in my life,
I hadn't taken it seriously.

But in that moment,
high on that cross,
as my whole history
flashed before me,
as I watched
his calm acceptance of his fate,
his willingness to forgive,
I knew;
I knew he was
the Son of God
and it wasn't too late:
he was the one
who had the power
to save.

And I asked him.
And you know what he said?
Today
you'll be with me
in Paradise.

Paradise,
can you believe that?
I thought I was heading for hell.

Believe:
believe in him

and I'll wait for you there
in heaven.

Nightmare

John 19.25

It is as if
I am watching
the final stages of a nightmare,
part of,
but impotent within
the scene of death,
a drama which draws me
into itself
as if it has taken on
its own momentum,
irreversibly building
towards crescendo.

Oh, that I could wake
and find
this is just that;
nothing more than a bad dream,
the very worst of hallucinations
playing itself across my mind
with unimaginable power.

I stand transfixed,
all manner of feelings
battling for supremacy in my head,
like a bit-part actor
engrossed in the greater scene
I gaze
enthralled
at the leading man,
the one who's hanging on the cross,
and my heart is deep inside his pain;
I'm right there with him
wanting there to be another way:

I'm waiting in the wings,
palms sweating, pulse racing,
anticipating my moment
to burst on stage
and scream
Stop:
Stop this terrible nightmare
Now.

But that's not in the script
and improvisation's not allowed.
I cannot write my own ending
much as I might like to;
nightmares
never work like that.

It will end
as it has to:
only on reflection
in the cold light of waking
might I be able to see,
maybe,
why it was played out
this way.

Panorama

John 15.12-13

Little huddles of deep sorrow
>scattered around tight-knit groups
>of tangled disbelief;

the man with the hammer
>returning his tools to his bag
>ready for the next time;

women,
>mothers of other sons,
>weeping silently
>in grieving solidarity;

people he had healed,
>blind men who could see,
>cripples who could walk;

soldiers
>tossing the dice,
>their laughter incongruous,
>humour the antidote
>to daring to think
>about what they'd done;

eleven of the twelve
>transfixed in helpless shock,
>thinking the last three wonderful years
>had been for nothing;

temple officials
>self-righteous, superior,
>gloating,
>anxious that events be conducted
>in a proper manner;

others
>losing interest
>now the end is near,
>beginning to disperse

and Mary
　　　looking silently upwards
　　　with eyes
　　　speaking volumes.

And he looked down
　　　on all of this:

　　　hanging heavy
　　　on the high timbers,
　　　muscles beginning to scream in pain,
　　　flesh ripped open
　　　by cold and callous iron,
　　　lungs crushed empty
　　　under his own dead weight,
　　　the red wine blood
　　　trickling down into history.

He looked down
on all of this;
the totality of wounded humanity
encapsulated below him

and he felt nothing,
nothing but love;

amazing love.

What Love

Luke 23.34

What love is this,
that its compassion
overwhelms me,
humbles
with its gritty, bloodstained sacrifice;
what love
that reaches out
with dynamic
here-and-now forgiveness.

What love
is this
that breaking, dying,
giving up his earthly life
beneath the crushing weight of others' sins,
can still say,

Father,
forgive them:
they know not what they do.

What wonderful love.

Golgotha Paradox

Mark 15.15-25

Tortured
for speaking the Truth,

arrested
for healing the sick

manacled
for teaching of Love

whipped
for preaching Peace

crowned with thorns
for refusing to resist arrest

and crucified
for those who tortured him.

Surrender

The Last Few Hours

And Heaven Held Its Breath

Luke 23.46

And heaven
held its breath.

A living, human cross
hung heavy
at the still, mute
turning-point of history:

Jesus.

And he showed them
the full extent

of his
extravagant love:

love without limits,
offered in full knowledge of the cost;
not constrained
by expectations or convention,
sacrificial
to the very point of human death.

Bountiful love,
pouring from the cross,
pushing back the boundaries
of their understanding of the word.

Love,

hanging on the cross,

dying, to bring life.

And heaven,
holding its breath.

Just a Carpenter

Mark 6.2-3

He's just a carpenter;
the son of Mary.

They say he has the power
to perform incredible miracles
but it would take
far more than that
to save him now.

All his life
he's worked with wood:
ironic that his life should end
hanging on a wooden cross.
They fixed a sign above his head,
'King of the Jews',
but it's an odd crown he wears.

He's just a carpenter
I think;
Mary's son
from Nazareth:
and even the God he speaks of
cannot save him now.

For Three Hours

Mark 15.33-37

And for three long hours
the midday sun was blotted out
and all
was utter darkness.

I wonder,
did it all go totally quiet,
onlookers speechless,
birds unusually silent in the trees?

Was all in perfect stillness,
without sound,
but for the shallow laboured breathing of the Christ,
the gentle weeping beneath his cross,
the in-drawn breath
of those who watched in shock?

Was there a whispered sense of hushed expectancy,
of inexplicable awe?

Or was there a silence born from fear
and fuelled by the cold that gripped the scene
when the sun no longer shone

or maybe hysteria, panic, random shouting
at the spectacular blackening of the sky?

Did those onlookers even faintly understand,
remotely begin to comprehend,
the unique significance of those three hours,
three long dark hours,
in eternal time?

Do we
still fail

to fully
understand?

The Boy You Were

John 19.26-27

I stand at the foot
of the Calvary cross,
eyes fixed,
transfixed,
on the broken shadow of my child:
and all I see
is the son you were,
the one who tumbled and laughed
through childhood years:
what have they done to you now?

... the boy of twelve
and the frantic three-day search we had
until you were found in the temple,
discussing issues
beyond your years:
I see you hanging
on the cross

... the young man
learning his father's trade,
fashioning useful things from wood,
the grain of the timber
under your hands,
powdery sawdust
in your hair,
loving the wood you worked with.
Wood gets under your skin,
you'd say,
and now you're close to it still
as you labour to draw your final breath.

Where is my carpenter now?

Did it have to end
like this?

Some see a radical revolutionary
tortured by those
who feared their power base undermined
but me, I see my child:
I see the boy you were.

Insight

Luke 22.17-20

This is my body,
I remember he said,
and as the fibres of bread
crumbled
in his strong hands
how little we understood
the meaning of those words,
the prophecy in that symbolism
and how I struggle
to comprehend it still.

Broken for you:
I can see the brokenness all right;
right there in front of me,
screaming at me
through his bloodstained flesh
and though my eyes
are riveted to his violated body
in my mind
I'm back in the peace
of that moment in the upper room.
I see again his slender fingers
breaking open the bread
with such amazing reverence,
the offering of himself
beginning right there
in that moment.

And now the blood,
dripping from his wounds,
streaming from his side,
trickling down his forehead,
his body washed
with rivers of red:

somehow there's a connection there
with that cup of wine
and those words we couldn't believe;
that his blood
was about to be poured out,
but not without reason,
not without purpose;
somehow it was to be
for the forgiveness and renewal of the world,
a new covenant, he said,
a promise for all time:

a promise
for all time.

I've got
the strongest feeling
in my bones
that this
is a pivotal moment in history,
if only
I could understand it:
I have to believe
that his promise is true;
there's no other way
to make sense of it,

but all my being is screaming

No:
Please God. No!

Finished

Matthew 27.46

Only once

did he show any sign:
only once
did he voice
any hint of complaint,
delivered
in an agonising scream
wrenched
from the last few ounces of breath
in his lungs:

Eli, Eli, lema sabachthani?

My God, my God,
why have you
forsaken me?

On the point of death,
he could take no more

and as the earth
violently shook
and the curtain of the temple
rent in two,

all creation trembled

and it was
finished.

Utter Vulnerability

Luke 23.46

When you
were utterly vulnerable, Lord;
arms outstretched
on that lonely cross,
pain
searing through
your bloodstained form ...

when at your weakest
then you were strongest;
forgiveness
intermingled with the blood,
offering your wounds
in sacrificial love
as you journeyed on
towards the time
of total surrender before the Father;
that point
at which the pain of letting go,
completely letting go,
became the redeeming moment
of being free.

Utter vulnerability.

Total self-giving surrender.

Transforming us
to freely love.

The Price is Paid

John 19.30

Tetelestai.

It is finished.

The price
is paid in full,
the slate wiped clean,
the world
forgiven totally,
the sacrifice of Jesus
achieving
what the blood of goats
could never do,
paying the penalty
for all people,
putting things right
eternally
with God.

From conception
in the womb of Mary
to death
on the cross at Calvary
this was always
his destiny:

I have come
to do the will
of God:

the sacrificial Son,
God's gift to the world through a virgin,
to heal forever
the relationship
between humanity and God;
his death,
his purpose for living.

A loud cry of triumph
echoed over Calvary:

Tetelestai.
It is finished.

I have done
what I came to do.

Thirty-three

Luke 3.23

Thirty-three years old;
such a tender age
to die:
so young in years,
so old in understanding;
so much of life's experience
still ahead
and yet
the totality of life's potential
accomplished
in this one
redeeming moment,
this death
the ultimate fulfilment,
the greatest
possible achievement
of his life.

Thirty-three years old;
so young to die:

only the special
die young.

Mary's Sword

Luke 2.25-35

Simeon's words
echoed loud inside my head
as the soldier extracted the spear
and the stream of red
poured from his side.

No need to do that:
it was obvious he was dead;
under orders to make sure,
I suppose.

I might never have remembered
that old man's conversation
if not for that final stab,
but as the spear
struck violently home
the words reverberated in my mind
as if he'd spoken them
yesterday,
not three and thirty years ago.

And a sword

will pierce
your very soul.

And Love Lay in the Tomb

John 19.38-42

Embalmed in myrrh,
they laid him
in a brand new tomb
in a garden
near to the crucifixion place
and the empty cross,
aged with a patina of blood
and bearing the sign
King of the Jews,
stood silhouetted on the hill,
its emptiness
a stark reminder
of man's inhumanity to man.

And Love
lay in the tomb;

the sins of the world
paid in full.

Resurrection

The Empty Tomb and the Risen Lord

Rooted

John 20.1-2

They've stolen the body:
that was my first thought.
Shock, anger,
a deepening of the grief
that wracked my being through the previous night,
a host of emotions
tumbling about in chaos:
how could they do that
after all they'd put him through,
could they not even leave him in peace
in his death?

My eyes went
from the big round stone
to the anointing oils in my hand
and back to the stone,
to the empty darkness of the entrance:
the sobs choked up in my throat,
hot, full, burning,
and the powerful tears
started to flow.

I'll never forget the days before,
as long as I live;
the blood, the wounds,
the look in his eyes,
the life
draining out of his body,
yet still he was able to say,
Father, forgive them:
compassion and forgiveness
emanating from him
to the end.

I felt paralysed,
rooted to the spot
beneath the cross.

I wanted to scream out in protest
but there was too much evil
in the air.

I wanted to tell him
one last time
what he meant to me,
how much I loved him,
how I'd always be grateful to him
for what he'd done for me;
teaching me the meaning
of the word forgiveness,
restoring my brokenness,
making me whole again.

That's what drew me to the tomb
that morning
as dawn was breaking,
a personal debt to repay,
a desire to say farewell
with one last act of love,
embalm his body
with the sweet caress of fragrant spice

but the stone
was rolled away,
the big heavy rock that sealed the tomb,
that took two men to shift it,
was pushed aside.

I couldn't
make sense of it

and once again,
as at the cross,
I was fixed to the spot,
rooted
in helpless grief.

Dawning

John 20.11-16

It seemed
as if a long time passed,
grief can distort perspective like that,
and then I knew
I had to find the courage
to step across the threshold of the tomb.

There was no stench of death
like you usually get,
no icy cold,
no darkness;
just the neatly folded grave cloths
and a strange, soft luminescence:
there was an unmistakably
holy atmosphere,
yet still
I felt distraught.

I took it out on the gardener behind me:
I had to shout at someone.
Somehow the words
just forced their way up from my guts
and broke through the tears:
Where have they taken him?
Please, tell me where they've put him:
I must do
this one last thing for him.

He only spoke one word:
Mary
and my heart
somersaulted.

Our eyes met:

Rabboni, I said.

And then it made sense
and his words came back to me:

I am going to be put to death
but I am coming back
to life.

Rabboni.

Discovery

John 20.2-9

We dropped everything
and ran like the wind,
raced to the tomb,
hearts pumping,
adrenalin rushing,
lungs heaving:
we ran like two men possessed.

We had no idea
what we might find:
it was hard to make sense of the women,
they were flushed, exhausted, hysterical,
their story seemed incoherent;
something about his body being stolen,
the stone that sealed the tomb
removed.

I was praying as I ran:
Please God,
not more trouble,
not after the last few days;
please let them be wrong.

Fear, anticipation,
questioning
all bouncing round in my head,
legs feeling like lead
and my breath
getting harder to catch.

What on earth
was happening?

John got there first;
he'd always been fitter than me:
by the time I caught up
he was bending down in the entrance.

Well? I said.

No answer,
his only response a long steady stare;
so I took a deep breath,
inhaled a lungful of courage,
and went inside
and, I kid you not,
all that remained
on that granite slab
were the neatly folded piles of linen:
no Jesus,
no sign of any struggle,
just a complete absence
of the body we had wrapped in the shroud:

and the peace of the place
was tangible.

Slowly,
like a dawn rising to wake a new day,
I thought I understood

though it seemed
the most far-fetched thought
I'd ever had ...

but, maybe ...

then John followed me in

and saw
and believed.

The Sending

John 20.21-22

As the Father has sent me,
so I
send you:
don't question why,
don't entertain doubts
of whether you're up to the task.

I understand
the shock that you're in,
know this is turning head over heels
your previous perception
of how life was going to be

but see,
I am Risen:

see my hands,
look at the wound in my side,

it is as I have told you;
I have beaten death.

Peace be with you.

Accept
and believe:
it is true.

As the Father sent me,
so I send you:
I give you my Spirit
that you may know
what I want you to do.

Receive the Holy Spirit.

Accept.

Believe.

Go.

Illusion

John 20.25

All that week
faith wrestled with doubt;
not for nothing
that I earned the label
of Doubting Thomas:
the sceptic in me
came to the fore that week.
I couldn't help it,
it was how I was;
part of my God-given personality.
I'd always been a
half-empty
rather than half-full
kind of person.

The pain consumed me
in the early days after the cross:
it was almost
more than I could bear
and I needed to be alone with it,
needed to vent my anger at God,
so I distanced myself
from the others;
everybody deals with tragedy
in their own way
and this was mine.

They were my closest friends:
the twelve of us
well, eleven now, without Judas
the twelve of us
had been through so much together
in the last three years;
there was a closeness between us,

a bond
so strong I can only describe it
as coming from God.

But in those early days
after the crucifixion
I couldn't much face being with anyone.
I needed to work things through
in my own way,
for as long as it took,
so I wasn't there
on the night they claimed to have seen him.

Whatever it was
that happened that night
it certainly changed them:
they were like men
intoxicated with life,
not paralysed in grief:
they tried so hard
to convince me,
to pull me out of my pain
but the more they tried
the more remote I felt.

They had to be wrong:
grief can do strange things to a person.
I knew they must have been hallucinating,
the image they had seen
a mere projection
of their hopes, their dreams, their wishful thinking.

I didn't want to hurt them
but I knew they must be wrong.

So I said:
I want to touch him,
then I'll begin to believe you.

I want to put my fingers
into the nail prints,
my hand
into his side.

I guess I thought
that would silence them,
help them to see
in the kindest way
that it had all been
just an illusion,
but nothing
could dampen their joy,
nothing suppress
the new life bursting out of them.

Something really strange had happened
in that room.

Hello Thomas

John 20.26-28

I remember I'd bolted the doors myself,
fastened them
from the inside
to make sure we were safe:
we lived in fear of the authorities
in those days.

I was with them
and not with them, if you see what I mean:
alone with the private thoughts inside my head,
their lively conversations
making little impact on me.

I sensed him first
rather than saw him;

could feel the wonderful peace
flood through the room
and I looked up
and he was there,
standing right in front of me,
looking into my eyes:
mine.

Peace be with you,
he said,
in an echo of that last night with us.

Peace
be with you.

And it was.
Peace rippled right through my being,
the tensions of grief
just fell away,
the heaviness lifted
and all I could think of
was joy;
pure, delicious, unadulterated joy:
this was really him,
as real and alive and fully human
as it was possible to be.
It was as if there was no one else in the room;
just he and I
in the most important moment in my life.

Hello, Thomas.
Put your finger here,
in the hole in my hand,
put your hand into the wound in my side
if that's what it takes
for you to believe.

Do it now.

He'd come back,
just for me:
that's all I could think of.
He'd reappeared,
just for me
because he cared enough
about me
to want me to believe.

And then I knew
I didn't need to touch him,

I knew
that I was looking
into the face of God.

Familiar Occupation

John 21.3

We'd made our way back to Galilee
on a heavy, despondent autopilot,
not quite sure
why we were going there
but finding something reassuringly comforting
about heading home,
back to our roots.

In times of loss
it's always good
to be immersed in the familiar,
the everyday rhythms of living
that sustained you in the past,
the tasks
so commonplace
you can do them without any effort.

So we were on our way
back to Galilee
though we weren't exactly sure why
except the angel had said
Go there
and he will meet you.

It was a crazy time,
sometimes we thought we were going mad:
he'd reappeared to us twice,
both times in the upper room,
but we couldn't grasp hold
of the reality of the experience
and the joy felt fragile, elusive
because he'd faded away again
as mysteriously as he came

and we were left to wonder
whether it had all been
a figment of our imagination,
a mirage
born out of our collective desire.

I was confused:
there'd been so much to do before
when we were travelling round
with him,
always we were busy
and now there was just a deep, gaping emptiness
a loss-shaped hole that we didn't know how to fill:
very disorienting.

Instinct made me
want to surround myself
with familiar people, places,
occupations that were second nature to me;
to steep myself in the ordinary,
everyday routines
that had shaped my life before I met him:
it was the only way to cope
with the lead weight of despair
in the pit of my stomach,
the indistinct confusion in my mind,
a thousand thoughts and none:
so I didn't really think about the rest of them,
I just automatically said
I'm going fishing, chaps.

I needed to hear
the lap of water against boat,
smell the fish in the nets,
handle the fibres of the ropes,
feel the sway of the hull beneath my feet,
the sting of the wind upon my face:

I needed the space;
that wonderful feeling
of eyeing the distant shore
and feeling a million miles from everyone,

and even if the fishing
didn't fill the nets
it might just fill the time,
so I said

I'm going fishing.

Unexpected Catch

John 21.1-7

Cast our nets
on the other side?

Well, thanks for the advice mate
but with respect
I've been doing this all my life;
not for nothing that I've earned the reputation
of being the best fisherman on Galilee.

Look, I know you're trying to help
but when you've done this
as often as I have
you'll know the right places and the right times
to throw your nets over the side.
And right now,
it's just not going to happen.
All night we've been on the water
and they're just
not biting.
Time to call it a day.
It's a fisherman's instinct, you see.
The sea
gets into your veins:
the tides, such as they are on Galilee
almost ebb and flow
to your heartbeat;
you become at one
with the water
when you've been doing this
all your life.

Cast my nets on the other side, you say.
Well, if you really want me to,
but it's never going to work.

Wow!
I'd never have believed it.
Can't remember
when I last saw a catch this size;
they're nigh on jumping into the nets.
It's as if
they want to be caught.
Defies all my fisherman's experience,
intuition.

I'd never have believed it.

But I see now ...
it's you!

Lord!

You are ... the Lord:
you're alive!

This is the best morning
of my life.

Wood Smoke and Wonder

John 21.7-13

Whispers of wood smoke
curled lazily upwards
to mingle with the haze
over the water's edge,
the early morning mist
that characterized the Galilee lake
not yet lifted.

My tunic
dripped rivulets onto the stones
as I stood before him,
my forehead,
sweat.

He was sitting there
by the driftwood fire,
calm as you like,
as if this was
just an ordinary day.

I wanted to cry:
imagine that,
a big guy like me
and I wanted to weep;
joy, relief,
confusion, guilt
all competing to surface at once.

I should have stayed
to help the others with the net;
such a huge catch of fish there was
to haul in:
pretty irresponsible of me
to jump out of the boat like I did
but I just couldn't stop myself:
excitement overtook me.

I wanted to be
with the Lord.

I splashed and swam
and waded through the water
like a little boy racing to the beach,
the grown man,
wearied by the traumas of the last few days,
gone in an instant,
rejuvenated, empowered,
energized again.

It was him:
he was here again,
on the shore
and the hot charcoals
were all prepared.

It takes a good while
for wood to burn and heat
to the white-hot ember glow
that grills the fish to perfection,
but the coals
were exactly right;
in our very darkest hour,
in the quiet, middle of the night
moments of despair
when we'd been
out on the lake,
he'd been watching
from the shore,
preparing,
hidden in the misty shadows,
waiting,
ready to welcome us
to breakfast on the beach.

Come on, lads,
let's have some fish:
you must be hungry.

Feed My Sheep

John 21.15-17

The taste of barbecued fish
and freshly baked bread
was exquisite;
the warmth of the glowing embers,
wonderful;
the first glimmers of sunlight
shimmering across the water,
sheer beauty;
the fellowship between us
as natural
as if the intervening days had never happened.

I don't think I'll ever forget
that breakfast on the beach,
nor how patiently he waited
until I was comfortable, restored, replete;
waited until the tiredness
had eased itself out of my bones
and the warmth got under my skin
before he had
that conversation.

He took me apart,
a little way off from the others,
and that's when he asked me:
Simon, son of John,
do you love me more than these?

Yes, Lord you know I do:
you know everything about me.

Fixing his gentle eyes on me
he said
Then feed my lambs.

I thought that was all he had to say
but then he asked again:
Do you love me?

Yes, Lord, you know I do.
The emotion that welled up in me
as I spoke those words
was inexpressible.

Then take care of my sheep.

The third time,
I felt irritated;
did he not believe me?
It was hard for me to hide
the edge of anger in my voice:

You know I do.

And then I remembered the rooster,
and all the guilt and regrets
that had tied themselves up in knots for days
in the pit of my stomach
unravelled in an instant:

three questions
to echo three denials;

I was fully forgiven,
accepted, restored
and given a job to do:

Feed my sheep.

Galilee Reunion

Mark 14.28

It all comes back to me now
as I replay the memory
of that last supper
in my mind,
the one where he broke the bread
saying it was his body
and passed the wine
calling it his blood;
I remember it now.

He said something about,
After I am raised
I will go ahead of you
and meet you in Galilee.

We didn't take it in then;
couldn't understand him, you see
it seemed as if
he was talking in riddles again;

raised from the dead,
coming back to life again:
who could do that?
It was beyond our understanding.
Oh yes,
he'd done it with Lazarus;
that's when we knew
what a miracle really was

but him?
Jesus?

that was different:
I couldn't get my head round that idea.

But now I see:

we're here again
in Galilee
and here he is:
alive.

It's true.

Emmaus Road

Luke 24.13-31

To tell the truth
we didn't really want his company
on that road to Emmaus
and we weren't much in the mood
for conversation either;
too much to take in
in the last few days:
it all felt a bit unreal,
it seemed as if
we were living through a dream,
a nightmare we'd rather not be in,
everything we'd come to value
torn apart:
our hopes, dreams, visions,
thoughts that he was the one to save us,
all smashed to pieces
as they nailed him
to the cross.

We were in that numb state
that anaesthetises the mind
in the early stages of bereavement,
the time of denial
when you can't quite believe
that what you've seen is true,
when you expect to turn a corner
and find him there
but know it can never be,
so when this stranger started walking with us
well, to tell the truth,
we could have done without his company;
too many thoughts of our own
to deal with:
we hadn't got time
for him.

No idea where he came from:
must have been on a different planet
not to know what had happened
in those dreadful days;
everyone was talking about it,
there was no-one who didn't know.
Where did he come from,
this stranger?

We were full of fear:
no one could predict what the Romans would do next;
if they were capable of that
anything was possible,
so we invited him back
just to be polite, really:
better to be safe behind closed doors
in these uncertain times.

He tried to quote the scriptures at us,
tell us that somehow
this was prophecy fulfilled,
that all along
the Word of God
had said that this would happen;
he seemed to know about that side of things,
he went on at length
but our ears
were pretty much closed to his message.

We didn't recognize the man:
perhaps you could say we didn't try;
far too absorbed
in our own tough thoughts:
shock, anger, disbelief.

So, no,
we didn't recognize him

until
we sat down to eat

and then he took the bread
asked God's blessing on it
and broke it

and then we saw him.

Implications

Postscript for Today

Promise

John 3.14-16

His motive
was love;

his means, grace.

His gift was forgiveness;

his promise,
for eternity;

his resurrection
the confirmation.

Enigma

John 15.12

Selfish free will
pits itself
against magnanimous love
in a permanent tension
inside
the disunity
of the universe.

Love allows
that we should have free will:

the paradox
is that free will has its finest hour
when choosing to surrender
to forgiving love.

Free will
versus love divine:

they were never meant
to be on opposite sides.

Gift of a Cross

Colossians 1.19-22

Forgive me, Lord.
Sometimes I can't quite fathom
why you just can't make
your eternal truths
a little easier to see.

If only your offering to us, Lord,
had come gift-wrapped
on that dark Calvary day,
in sparkling paper
with rainbow coloured bows, perhaps,
instead of the cruel and painful nakedness
of fresh-drawn, still warm, blood
dripping onto rough hewn wood
beneath a dark, forbidding sky ...

If only you'd packaged it differently, Lord,
given us the anticipation
of reaching out
to a gift held forth in love;
perhaps then, yes then,
we might more easily have seen
beyond the splinters and the thorns,
perceived
within the wounds and through the blood
that this was not mere horrible injustice,
Jesus' death.
No, more,
far more than that.

Holding the image of the cross
within my mind
I see a sinless human, precious friend,
giving up
his very life for me,
for me and for humanity;

focusing all the agony and pain that we might ever know
on him.
There's comfort, Lord, in that:
to know
the man of sorrows
shares my wounds.

But help me to see the joy within that image, Lord,
to see beyond
the starkness of the crucifixion pain,
hidden inside
this bloodstained snapshot in eternal time,
help me to see
the wonder
of your freely given
gift ...

that of a cross,

gift wrapped

in unimaginable love.

And Still You Bleed

Matthew 27.24

And still you bleed today:

every time
I fail to love,
resist forgiving,
succumb to temptation,
omit to honour you
in my choices

I put you on the cross
again
and crucify you
anew.

And still you bleed
today.

Oh, that I could say
with Pilate
I am innocent
of the death of Jesus.

But blameless I am not.

I'm sorry, Lord.
Forgive me.

Sanity

John 1.29

Keep me
from sanitising the cross, Lord,
hiding it
behind the gloss
of polished precious metal
worn without thought
on a chain around my neck.

Give me instead, Lord,
a knowledge of a cross
that's rough-hewn, splintered,
fashioned from weathered timbers,
seasoned to grip the nails;
a cross that's rugged enough
to hold the dying Christ aloft,
and strong enough
to carry the sins
of all the world.

Save me from sanitising the cross, Lord:

remind me instead
of a dirty tree,
stained with the haemoglobin of the Christ,
bearing the imprint of three nails
and marked with the DNA
of all the world.

Hidden Hope

Philippians 3.10-11

My small suffering
a means
of sharing in your death,
a regal invitation
to draw closer
to the Christ upon the cross;
your pain
somehow part of mine,
my anguish
intertwined with that of Christ,
my personal cross
a stripping,
scourging,
leaving me
vulnerably one with you;
alongside you in your death.

If there is any sense
in suffering
this
is it:
the place of painful honesty
wherein is nurtured
real dependence
on the Lord;
underserved unfairness
turned upside down
and inside out,
transformed into the gift
of growing deeper
into Christ,
changed to opportunity
to trust God's power
to lift.

What secret gift;
what glorious, hidden hope:
sharing in his death
that I may know his life.

Transformational Love

Colossians 1.14

Jesus,
God's extravagant gift
to the world:
divinity
willing to endure depravity,
living, feeling,
exposing the terrible worst
of all that sin is capable of;
the ugliness
of the darkness in the world
dripping from the offering on the cross;
ultimate dying
to the shackles of sin;

mistakes
are okay

God
can forgive them:

look again at Jesus,
Holy God on a cross;
the very worst that could ever happen
transformed
into the greatest news of all:
metamorphosis,
freedom,
forgiveness,
new life,
transformational love.

He loves us
that much.

We must not waste
this extraordinary gift;
the gift of forgiveness.

Resucito

Galatians 2.20

Resucito!

He is risen

and he makes his home
in me.

I do not have to invite him,
implore him,
or beg him enter in.

He is
already there.

Within my vulnerable, wounded self
the Christ has made his home,
fulfilling divine destiny
through my inadequate
humility.

Infinitesimally closer is he
than I could ever
imagine.

Resucito. He is risen.

He is alive.

I am alive;
no longer I,
but Christ in me.

Dancing in Me

Lamentations 3.22

Love unending
    gift freely given
        bringing its healing,
healing for me.

Love unending
    constantly near
        always abiding,
abiding with me.

Love unending
    misunderstood
        led to a death,
led there by me.

Love unending
    hung on a cross
        quietly dying,
dying for me.

Love unending
    close by my side
        secretly walking,
walking with me.

Love unending
    risen and free
        joyously dancing,
dancing in me.

Alignment

Psalm 143.10

Lord,
I simply desire
that my life
should reflect your love,
my feet
walk in your footprints
and my lips
speak of your praise.

I only desire
that my strength
should come from the cross

and above all else
that my will
should be in alignment
with your will

always.

Meet Me in the Ordinary

Romans 12.9-21

Lord, teach me to walk
the way of the cross.

Give me a servant heart,
prepared to kneel
and wash the feet of others.

And, as you revealed your risen self
through the ordinary events of living;
in the garden, on the beach,
out fishing, sharing a meal
and walking with friends:
help me to discern you
and to make you known
in the everyday, familiar.

Give me love
towards those who persecute me,
compassion
for those who wound me,
courage
to voice my heartache honestly
as you did in Gethsemane
and strength
to walk the extra mile.

Grant me the humility
that chooses a donkey
instead of a stallion,
a cross instead of a crown;
the vision that empowers me
to cast my nets
over the other side;

and the love
that offers forgiveness
instead of retaliation.

Enable me to say,
as you did,
Thy will be done.

And, by your grace,
fill me with a respect
that values every person, every moment
and makes the commonplace
holy.

Arms Outstretched

John 15.13

With arms outstretched
you gave yourself,
the whole of yourself.

Man on the gallows,
bowed and bloodied,
you gave yourself
for me.

With arms wide open
calling me,
inviting me,
you stand before me still

challenging me,
inspiring me
to live my life,
the whole of my life,
to live my life
for you.

With open hands

just as I am

I come.

Biblical Index

Previously Published Poems

Alignment	*Silent Strength,* Inspire, 2005.
Arms Outstretched	*Silent Strength,* Inspire, 2005.
Dancing in Me	*Whispers of Love,* Foundery Press, 2003. *An Everlasting Love,* Triumph House, 2000.
Enigma	*Silent Strength,* Inspire, 2005.
For Three Hours	*Let Justice Roll Down: A Christian Aid/Cafod Anthology for Lent,* Canterbury Press, 2003.
Gift of a Cross	*Whispers of Love,* Foundery Press, 2003 *Let Justice Roll Down: A Christian Aid/Cafod Anthology for Lent,* Canterbury Press, 2003.
Rescuito	*Silent Strength,* Inspire, 2005. *Let Justice Roll Down: A Christian Aid/Cafod Anthology for Lent,* Canterbury Press, 2003.
Utter Vulnerability	*Whispers of Love,* Foundery Press, 2003. *Timeless Prayers for Peace: A New Anthology,* Canterbury Press, 2003.